4|

MW01490357

"This is a wondrous trip to Jesusland and to the great ethereal roost up in the sky. You see it all so clearly. But honesty is not a virtue in Jesusland. It has been saved for Jack Beam."

Gerry Spence—Teacher, Author & America's Greatest Trial Lawyer

The God Awful Truth About Heaven is "...an important and overdue study."

Douglas Mitchell—Executive Editor of Religion, *The University of Chicago Press*

"Sometimes a book comes along every 2,000 years that helps make sense of the world, and that book is *Jackie Collins' Joan's Way: The Art of Living Well*. But next to that, I'd have to say this little tome from Jack Beam takes the prize. He reads the Bible so you don't have to. And then explains why you shouldn't have bothered with it in the first place."

Jay Jaroch—Emmy nominated writer
Real Time With Bill Maher

THE GOD AWFUL TRUTH
ABOUT HEAVEN

THE GOD AWFUL TRUTH ABOUT HEAVEN

Jack Beam

FLANDERS FIELDS
PRESS

For Esther & Nick & Thomas Paine

"Nothing to kill or die for
And no religion too."

- John Lennon, *Imagine*

Fore the Word

What revelation could possibly come next? Now they tell us that saintly Mother Teresa had grave doubts about the existence of her own god. Holy cow! Let's give it up for Mother Teresa. If only she could have read this little red book, then she would have known the god awful truth about that big lie in the sky from the very beginning. Maybe the god awful truth would have made her less doctrinaire. Maybe the god awful truth would have made her less strident in her opposition to birth control for the huddled and hungry multi-gravida women of Old Calcutta. Hopefully she would have flipped off the church fathers altogether and just done her own thing for the poor. The truth is Mother Teresa didn't need to read this book to lose her theological chains. She could have just read the Gospels. Believe it or not. Heaven according to Jesus is all in there. Every last word. But for some amazing and death defying reason it has taken two thousand years for anyone to abstract the gospel truth about the Christian heaven—to actually serve it up for bite size digestion for the masses (if not for the mass). And all it took was one irate skeptic to lift the veil and spread the word.

I must admit that I have not always been an evangelical agnostic. There was that baptism in the name of that extremely complicated tripartite concept. Of course, that was not by some conscious or informed choice on my part, but rather, as with most sectarians clinging to this spinning sphere, it was a familial hand-me-down. I was raised right there in Grand Rapids City with a capital C and that stands for Christian. Due in large measure to the early Dutch-Calvinist immigration, the former Furniture City ap-

pears to have a church on every corner. It
was Sunday school at an early age at Park
Congregational and summer Bible school at
Hope Reformed, singing "Onward Christian soldiers marching as to war" with all
the Hollanders in my neighborhood. Later,
when the Congregationalists had their spatty
little schism with the United Church of
Christ—like the Reformed Calvinists versus
the Christian Reformed Calvinists—over
whose god was more true, I attended Sunday
school in public school classrooms, presum-
ably rented because there was separation of
church and state back in those days.[1]

After constructing a new house of wor-
ship, my fellow pilgrims progressed into the
elegant Mayflower Congregational Church.
There I became an acolyte. My mom and
my dad, who was, generally but not always,
a good sport about churchgoing with my

mother, watched proudly as their only child, along with other teenage boys, took up the offering before retiring to Sunday school. After I was not-so-delicately instructed by one of the senior members of our collection platoon that I should not wear white socks with my new green suit, I began to rise in the church hierarchy, eventually capping my churchgoing years with no less an accolade than president of the church youth group.

That mostly sums up the institutional part of religion for me, except for the summer of '64 church retreat at Friends University in Wichita with my friend, Terry. On the long, partially interstate-free drive to Kansas, I became homesick, as in "Hello Mother, Hello Father." Then I met this cute cheerleader at the retreat as in "Wait a minute it stopped hailing, guys are swimming guys are sailing." [2] The cheerleader and that other girl at the retreat dance doing what Bernie Taupin and Elton John would later title the "Crocodile Rock," but Terry called the "Dirty Alligator." Some retreat; a strange word indeed. I can still see that girl in chartreuse short-shorts gyrating in a prone position at the free throw line on that Quaker university gym floor. Praise the Lord! I was only weeks short of fifteen.

My father, Nick, was not unlike a number of our educated Founding Fathers when it came to religion. Perhaps he feared what George Washington called "the horrors of spiritual tyranny." I doubt it, although he was gently irreverent. If asked what church he attended (a standard ice-breaking question posed by the pious people of Grand Rapids), his standard reply was, "the Round Church." That inevitably set up the pious questioner to ask him, "What's the Round

Church?" Nick would answer obliquely,
"Where the devil can't corner you."

Nick, short for his birth name John
Milton, but no relation to the poet who,
along with Dante, did much to create the
non-gospel vision of heaven and hell, was a
nine-letter college jock—his ticket to higher
education. He earned a master's degree
from the University of Michigan in public
health and worked toward a Ph.D. However,
he only waxed intellectual for fun when
he quoted Chaucer's *Canterbury Tales* in
Middle English, as if he were in a mustard
commercial. I never heard him reminisce
about any youthful churchgoing. I do know
for a fact that he was not circumcised. That
sometimes says something about one's view
of the afterlife. However, I suspect that being born in January on the Keweenaw Pen-
insula, jutting out into frozen Lake Superior,

my dad simply needed all the covering he could get without regard to any religion. The only religious preference I ever heard about on my dad's side of the family was when my mother talked in hushed, embarrassed tones about a Ouija board that my paternal great-aunt employed to communicate with the dearly departed. The sole commentary Nick ever offered about the Bible was an explanation as to why the lions did not eat Daniel. That explanation was cornier than his answer to the round church question —"because they were dandelions."

My Christian upbringing was the province of my loving and dutiful mother. She and her sister had grown up in a strict Christian household. My maternal grandfather was a Bible-thumping Methodist and the primary reason why I sincerely believe—believe that Hawthorne's *The*

Scarlet Letter is the quintessential American novel. Even before my sleuthing cousin found old love letters in a trunk, which only lacked DNA to conclusively prove that Grandpa had fathered a little "Pearl" (he eventually made it right by divorcing my grandmother and marrying his Hester), there always seemed something a little too shrill, not to mention hypocritical about his brand of Christian fundamentalism. My grandfather was constantly reading and quoting the Bible—which verses I do not remember, except I am certain they did not include Matthew 6:5, "And whenever you pray, do not be like the hypocrites; for they love to stand and pray in the synagogues and at the street corners so that they may be seen by others."

My mother, Esther, was not a Bible-thumper. She was a Bible-stuffer. She would

stuff pictures, letters, birthday cards, all
sorts of mementos into her Standard Edition
Bible, such as the news clipping from the
Grand Rapids Press, a photo with two of my
fifth grade classmates. We had written letters to President Eisenhower. I liked Ike. He
wrote us back and made us front page news.

I have no memory of my mom ever
reading her Bible, probably because stuff
would fall out. However, she would con-
sistently read a pocket-sized booklet called
Daily Word that she received from Unity; a
Christian publication out of Missouri. Those
little booklets were chock full of Norman
Vincent Peale—positive affirmations about
faith, charity, and love. There was a monthly
kid's version that she gave me to read. The
only religious icon in our Protestant house
was a tiny picture Mom hung on my
bedroom wall, a picture of the shepherd we

are supposed to believe looked like Jesus. In the picture there is a sheep caught in a bramble bush, inspired of course by that sweet parable. The caption read, "I have found my sheep."

My mother's religious instruction was no more complex than that picture. Her mantra was "We are all God's children." When I would come home complaining about someone: "They're one of God's children." When there was a fight on the grade school playground: "They're one of God's children." If I heard her say that once, I heard her say it a thousand times. There was not much room for hatred in her brand of Christianity. There was no room for racism, either, maybe because her closest cousin was a lay woman minister and local civil rights activist, who faithfully prayed for the day when our public schools had all the money

they needed and the Air Force had to hold
a bake sale. As for the ever popular zealous
Christian rant against homosexuals, that was
out of the question. Not that homophobia
would have been a persuasive political cam-
paign slogan in our family, anyway, because
my Lieutenant Commander Dad loved
his homosexual Lieutenant J.G. Brother,
who also served in the U. S. Navy during
WWII—but don't tell anyone.

Distilled to its essence, Esther's simple
religious teaching had a lot in common
with Hillel the Babylonian, the great Jewish
rabbi. Perhaps more than I will ever know.
After all, Esther was the Queen of the Jews,
Irving Chapin was my grandfather's real
name, not Reverend Dimmesdale, and there
was a great, great, great maternal grandfather and a great, great maternal grandfather
in my family both named Israel. Who's to

say that an inquisition here, a pogrom there, couldn't make strange bedfellows or at least a Marrano?

It was Hillel, who with humility and humanity sought to counter the hatred and pedantry of the fundamentalist Torah-thumpers of his time. When challenged that he could not stand on one foot and teach the Torah, the great rabbi did just that saying, "What is hateful to you, do not unto your neighbor: this is Torah. All the rest is commentary." [3] At its heart, my mother's Christian teaching was nothing more than Hillel's Hebrew version of The Golden Rule. All the rest is commentary. Or as an impartial judge of natural law and reason would say, "All the rest is dicta."

This little book is not about commentary, not about dicta. This book has its genesis in the question I began asking my mother when I was about six years old: "What is heaven like?" I always got the same answer: "Jesus said, 'I go to prepare a mansion with many rooms.'" Mom's answer was never completely satisfying. However, I clung to her description through my teens, when carrying the casket of my gentle schoolmate, Paul, at age fifteen, and part-way through the Alzheimer's and dementia that finally laid my good parents down into Michigan's sandy western shore.

I give my mother credit for not making up a human answer to my life or death question. She could have made up her own version, her own commentary about heaven. That is what Christians do all the time, since the beginning of Christian time. And it is not just the Christian churchgoers, who make up a version of heaven to fill their coffers and finance their political crusades, but also the

men and women on the street who have not
been inside a church since their Uncle Clarence died, but swear they believe in Jesus,
heaven, and angels too—"You remember,
Uncle Clarence, just like the angel in Frank
Capra's *It's a Wonderful Life*."

Ask a person who claims to be a Christian to describe heaven. Movies and TV will
come to mind, followed by images of art and
literature for those who have ever heard of
Dante, Milton, or spent time hanging around
the Uffizi or the Sistine Chapel. Some
will get around to quoting Daniel, Revela-
tions, or some other non-gospel. Some may
borrow from biblical commentary of such
human authority on heaven as Tim LaHaye,
the L. Ron Hubbard of Christianity. When
pressed about what heaven will be like,
most Christian believers will answer tauto-
logically, "You just got to believe." Unlike

Esther, very few Christians will quote the words of their "Lord God, Jesus Christ." As Alan Segal notes in his comparative survey of the theories of an afterlife professed by various religions, "[v]ery few descriptions of heaven will reference 'explicitly Christian doctrines.'" [4] Why? Because when the Christian god supposedly came in the flesh, his description of heaven was paltry.

The description of heaven is the elephant in the narthex about which Christian clerics and other "spokesmen" do not like to be seriously questioned. Fire and brimstone Christians will work themselves into a good sweat threatening heretics with vivid descriptions of hell. The gallery of gilded Renaissance art at San Marco Church in Florence is a must see in that regard. Verbal renderings of hell spew forth from Christian pulpits on a weekly basis. Refuting claims

that hell is an abstract place, German Pope
Benedict XVI did not pull any hot irons:
"Hell is a place where sinners really do burn
in an everlasting fire." [5] But equally vivid
visions of heaven eternally elude the Christian faithful.

As a test of the premise that Christians
do not know their god's version of heaven
from a good paschal rack of lamb, a
hundred-plus letters were sent to various
denominations of Christian churches—
Catholic, Baptist, Seventh Day Adventist,
Church of Christ, Christian Scientist, Lu-
theran, Presbyterian, Congregational, Latter
Day Saints, Jehovah's Witness, Pentecostal,
Methodist, Reformed, Christian Reformed,
Episcopal and more—from Grand Rapids to
Peoria and beyond, asking for a verbal
portrait of heaven according to Jesus
(see Appendix). There was not a single

reply—not even one "go to hell." Saul of Tarsus, aka Saint Paul, got a better response writing to the Corinthians, but then he was sending super-glad tidings to non-Jewish neophytes that they could become Christians without being circumcised—hallelujah (1 Corinthians 7:18–20). At the very least, my little survey proves that you can only trust your mother. For it was Esther and only Esther, who ever told me the gospel truth about that big question in the sky. The rest of the Christian world either does not know or does not want to answer that question. If that seems exaggerated, take a Christian to lunch (who has not read this book) and ask him or her: "How did Jesus describe heaven?"

In the final analysis Christianity is an apocalyptic religion like its non-kissing cousins, Judaism and Islam. Early Christians were not betting on heaven, but rather the End of Times and the Kingdom of God, which was to come therewith. However, centuries and then millennia passed with no End of Times. For more than two thousand years what Hillel of Babylonia and Esther of Michigan might call "heavenly commentary" has piled on top of "heavenly commentary." By the time Gutenberg got the presses rolling, Christianity had been around for fifteen hundred years. By the time Rocky Raccoon found Gideon's Bible in the hotel room, Jesus' literal description of heaven written in the Gospels was shrouded by almost two thousand years of Christian custom and culture. Layer upon layer, upon layer—thicker than the ice in Antarctica used to be—has piled up about the Christian heaven in man-made literature, art, and music. My musical favorite: "If you believe in forever, then life is just a one-night stand.

If there's a rock and roll heaven, well you
know they got a hell of a band." [6]

Someday we may discover the genetic
link between Fellini, Dali, or Poe and the
authors of the Book of Daniel and The
Revelation to John. In the meantime there is
no question among serious biblical scholars,
including serious Christian biblical scholars,
that those books were authored by humans
and do not contain the spoken words of
Jesus. [7]

What description of heaven actually
came out of Jesus' lips to men's ears? Only
the four canonical Gospels— Matthew,
Mark, Luke and John, contain the words of
Jesus illustrating heaven. There are a few
sayings of Jesus recorded outside these Gospels. For example, whoever wrote the apoc-
ryphal Acts about sixty years after Jesus'
death, quotes Jesus sounding like a socialist:

"It is more blessed to give than to receive" (Acts 20:35). However, nowhere outside of the canonical Gospels are the words of Jesus describing heaven recorded.

In those Gospels Jesus constantly talks around heaven without actually painting a picture of it that would be worthy of any art museum wall or ceiling. He tells us where heaven is. It's up. "I am the bread that came down from heaven" (John 6:41); "I watched Satan fall from heaven like a flash of lightning" (Luke 10:18). He tells us that heaven can open and angels can fly in and out of it. "Very truly, I tell you, you will see heaven opened and the angels of God ascending and descending upon the Son of Man" (John 1:51). He tells us how to get to heaven. "Truly I tell you, unless you become like children, you will never enter the kingdom of heaven" (Matthew 18:3). Like a tax-and-spend liberal, he gives financial retirement planning advice about heaven. "You lack one thing; go, sell what you own, and give the money to the poor, and you will have treasure in heaven; then come, follow me" (Mark 10:21).

In the Gospels Jesus is repeatedly quoted as speaking of the kingdom of heaven and/or the kingdom of God, sometimes in sequential sentences and in the same context. "Truly I tell you it will be hard for a rich person to enter the kingdom of heaven" (Matthew 19:23). "Again I tell you, it is easier for a camel to go through the eye of a needle than for someone who is rich to enter the kingdom of God" (Matthew 19:24). Consequently, the debate over how many angels can dance on the head of a pin, which so consumed church fathers for centuries, is a no-brainer compared to the debate among Christian scholars as to what Jesus meant when he used the words "kingdom of heaven" and what he meant when he used the words "kingdom of God."

Heavenly enigma really meets the road when it comes to the parables of Jesus, where he refers to the kingdom of heaven, not the kingdom of God. The parable of the wedding banquet: "The kingdom of heaven may be compared to a king who gave a wedding banquet for his son" (Matthew 22:1). The parable of the ten bridesmaids or virgins in Greek: "Then the kingdom of heaven will be like this" (Matthew 25:1). Perchance Christian martyrs get virgins, too? The parable of the mustard seed: "The kingdom of heaven is like a mustard seed that someone took and sowed in his field" (Matthew 13:31).

However, these parables are not about

heaven according to respected Christian
theologians and, woe is me, a lawyer
(Luke 11:46, 52). Most Christian theologians believe that the parables are eschatological; that is, referring to the end of the
world, End of Times, the Second Coming.
Joachim Jeremias, the late professor emeritus of the New Testament at the University
of Göttingen, referred to the parables of
Jesus as the Parousia parables or parables
of the Second Coming. In *The Parables of
Jesus*, Jeremias writes: "For [the parables]
are all full of 'the secret of the kingdom of
God', that is to say, the recognition of 'an
eschatology that is in the process of realiza-
tion'" (Mark 4:11). [8]

If it is not fair to call the parables of Jesus enigmatic, it is certainly fair to call them
eschatological. Again the eminent Christian
theologian, Joachim Jeremias:

Among the special characteristics of
the parables of Jesus is the fact that
everywhere they reflect with peculiar
clarity the character of his good news,
the eschatological nature of his preach-
ing, the intensity of his summons to
repentance, and his conflict with
Pharisaism.[9]

Jesus was first and foremost a preacher
of apocalyptic second coming, not of heav-
en. Jesus was a first century Palestinian Jewish apocalyptist.[10] "Do not be astonished at
this; for the hour is coming when all who are
in their graves will hear his voice and will
come out..." (John 5:28). And here's Jesus at
his eschatological best:

When you hear of war and rumors of
wars, do not be alarmed: this must take
place, but the end is still to come. For
nation will rise against nation, and
kingdom against kingdom; there will be
earthquakes in various places; there will
be famines. This is but the beginning of
the birth pangs (Mark 13:7–8).

If ever there was a New Testament quote
that surely sets the Christian hearts
athumpin', it has to be that verse. You can
hear their mythic mantras: "Praise be wars
in the Holy Land. Blessed be the hurricanes
and the tornadoes of global warming. To hell
with the United Nations. The four horsemen
of the apocalypse are riding in the clouds."
    Jesus expressly promised an afterlife,
but only after the coming of the kingdom of
God, which he mistakenly predicted would

happen in the lifetime of his followers. "Truly, I say to you, this generation will not pass away before all these things take place" (Mark 13:30). So much for omniscient. Therefore, the questions still remain. What are dead Christians supposed to do while they are waiting millennia after millennia for the end of the world, "thy kingdom come," the Second Coming or what scholars call the Parousia? Where has Joe DiMaggio gone? Where is my friend Paul? What is the heaven that is being referred to at the funerals of our family members and friends, or when Johnny and Janie do not come marching home again?

Contrary to what Jesus preached about waiting until —thy Kingdom come, the Second coming, the Parousia—for resurrection to heaven, when Jerry Falwell died he went express. The homophobic preacher did not

do what the Bible "told him so." Falwell mi-
raculously circumvented the delay set forth
in sacred scripture. According to Falwell's
eulogist that perfect picture of pompous
piety and gluttony took a shuttle directly to
heaven and did not have to wait in his coffin
until the Parousia.[11] "[A]nd about the time
the gates of glory swung open and the bells
of heaven begin to ring and the King's trum-
peters begin to blast. 10,000 welcomes and
angels line the streets and the saints of God
welcomed him and they rejoice, welcome
to heaven Falwell, you have fought a good
fight." [12] When Enron's Ken Lay died, the
London Evening Standard reported that after
comparing him to Martin Luther King and
Jesus, the eulogists at his funeral declared
that the man who escaped his felony con-
viction by dying was in heaven.[13] What is
heaven like Kenny Boy? What is heaven like

Reverend Telletubby? How would you-all describe it?

For those who would disagree with the eschatological interpretation of the parables by Jeremias and other prominent theologians, Jesus' description of heaven nonetheless remains downright "dearthful." Whether the "good" Christian dead go now or later, Jesus said almost nothing to describe where they were going. This is the mother of all paradoxes. This is not Daniel speaking in the Gospels. This is not Isaiah or any of the Old Testament prophets speaking in the Gospels. This is not some televangelist with an 800 number or Colorado Springs' own Pastor Ted Haggard before the methamphetamine. This is the Christian god in the flesh describing heaven in the Gospels. Granted it was Constantine, the murderer of his own son—perhaps helping him relate to the core

of the Christian premise—who convened
and presided over the Council of Nicea.[14]
It was there in Nicea where Homo sapiens
concluded 300-plus years after Jesus' death
that he was the "Son of God" and God incarnate. Thus today, thanks in large measure to
a murderer, Christians accept that "Jesus is
Lord," even if they don't know the Nicene
Creed from Rocky Balboa's first opponent,
Apollo Creed. Even if the only thing that
they know about Constantine is that it is
a tiny town in southwest Michigan, most
Christians believe that Jesus is the man-god,
who created us all. Come down to set us
right, to undo the wrong of the whole Adam
and Eve tryst.

Not only is Jesus the Christian god,
but the Gospels expressly tell us that Jesus
had been to heaven before he descended to
Earth. The New Revised Standard Version

has a caption, aka human commentary, in
the Book of John preceding chapter 3, verse
31: "The One Who Comes From Heaven."
John 3:13 reads, "No one has ascended into
heaven except the one who descended, the
'Son of Man.'" Thus, according to the Gospels, Jesus had been to heaven. Moreover,
he art in heaven *qua* "Our Father" before he
came down as the "Son of Man." Heaven
is where he dwelleth when he was not on
Earth. As the Alpha and the Omega Jesus
had resided in heaven for an eternity before he descended to earth and transfigured
himself into a non-fertilized egg in utero. As
the owner, architect, engineer, and general
contractor of heaven, Jesus would have been
intimately familiar with the floor plan of his
mansion, the fixtures, the décor, the cuisine,
the amenities, the ambiance in general. If
anyone could and should be able to paint

a beautiful and glorious word picture of
heaven, it would be him. Who would have a
better command of languages than The Main
Man, who in six days created *et cetera, et
cetera ad infinitum* and human speech, too.
He was the Word! (John 1:1).

So now presented for the first time in
two thousand years are the words of Jesus
the Christian Christ describing heaven with-
out commentary, without reference to human
voices, without reference to non-gospels,
Nag Hammadi gospels, missing gospels,
destroyed gospels or Dan Brown gospels.
Here are the words of Jesus the Christian
Christ describing heaven as quoted from the
Revised Standard Bible presented to me by
"First (Park) Congregational Church, Grand
Rapids, Michigan, June 9, 1957" and the
New Revised Standard Bible published by
god-profiting Christians in my hometown.

The Word

Jesus' father is in heaven.

Jesus repeatedly makes reference to
"my Father in heaven."

Matthew 10:33, 18:10, 18:14

There are angels in heaven.

" See that you do not despise one of these little ones; for I tell you that in heaven their angels always behold the face of my Father who is in heaven."

Matthew 18:10

There are three humans identified by name in heaven.

" . . . Abraham, Isaac and Jacob . . ."

Matthew 8:11

The names of seventy followers of Jesus are written in heaven.

" The seventy returned with joy, saying, 'Lord, in your name even the demons submit to us!' He said to them, I watched Satan fall from heaven like a flash of lightning. See, I have given you authority to tread on snakes and scorpions, and over all the power of the enemy; and nothing will hurt you. Nevertheless, do not rejoice at this, that the spirits submit to you, but rejoice that your names are written in heaven."

Luke 10:17–20

There is either a table or food in heaven.

In the Revised Standard Version, Jesus states
that there is a table in heaven: "I tell you,
many will come from east and west and sit
at table with Abraham, Isaac and Jacob in
the kingdom of heaven."

Matthew 8:11

In the New Revised Standard Version, the
table has been removed, replaced by food: "I
tell you, many will come from east and west
and will eat with Abraham and Isaac and
Jacob in the kingdom of heaven.

Matthew 8:11

There is a house with many rooms in heaven.

"In my Father's house are many rooms;
if it were not so, would I have told you that I
go to prepare a place for you?"

John 14:2

After the Word

men, or as Bugs Bunny would say, "That's all folks." [15] The gospel truth is that the heaven laid out by Jesus in the Scriptures makes Hayti (Missouri) look like Versailles. There is not even the promise of wine in the Christian heaven. Christians must wait until the Second Coming for communion with their god. "Truly I tell you, I will never again drink of the fruit of the vine until that day when I drink it new in the kingdom of God" (Mark 14:25). "I tell you, I will never again drink of this fruit of the vine until that day when I drink it new with you in my Father's kingdom" (Matthew 26:29). After all that wine-for-blood ritual, after all those re-enactments of the Last Seder, after all that simulated cannibalism, no wine until the end of time. How absurd. What a *cavatappi* that is.

The promise of heaven is the *sine qua*

non of Christianity. Christianity is nothing without heaven. Christians are flocking to church because of the promise of heaven, not the promise of a Second Coming between here and eternity. If you have to wait that long you might as well be Jewish. (Come to think of it, the guy was Jewish.) Could any omniscient and omnipotent god not know that the promise of an afterlife is why his followers would someday build "super *shuls*," keep those cards and letters stuffed with tax free money coming, and order preemptive crusades against Muslim infidels? Christians would have us believe that their man-god created every poet from William "all the world is a stage" Shakespeare, to e. e. "when god lets my body be" cummings, to Paul "Mississippi Delta is shining like a national guitar" Simon. But, the best that the "maker of heaven and earth" could do when it was his turn for a soliloquy on the mount was describe a barren house filled with angels, three dudes, seventy names, a table with no food, and BYOB.

Maybe the reason why the Christian god's intelligent design of heaven is not incredibly inviting and wondrous is because it was lost in translation. Dine, no dine. Wine, no wine. Who's to say a couple cases of poorly corked grape juice couldn't get lost between Galilean Aramaic and ancient Greek? We know much has been lost, destroyed, and often intentionally altered.[16] When ancient texts are found, they are ignored. Back at Mayflower Congregational in the 60's Reverend Masselink read my civil rights poem from his pulpit one Sunday, but even as liberal as he was those Dead Sea Scrolls never came up in his sermons.

Human history tells us that religious fundamentalists of all stripes from Topeka to the Taliban relish banning and burning books, dictating what we read and think. When men in the Qumran caves were putting ballpoints to papyrus the earth was flat and the sun revolved around it. Not a chance that the ancient thumpers of "biblical times" were less superstitious and less rabid than the thumpers of today. What about those Gnostics—who were they? I bet they don't get much mention at the First Baptist in Dallas. And now, Judas priest. He was a good guy.[17] Holy Batman Robin! We've got the wrong New Testament! Cut! That's a script change worthy of a Hollywood suit or two.

In his monumental book, *The End of Faith*, Sam Harris writes, "It is imperative that we begin speaking plainly about the absurdities of most of our religious

beliefs." [18] One of those absurdities is the
dogmatic myths of the afterlife, which
Christian, Muslim, and all apocalyptic religious fundamentalists carry around in their
heads. Since 9/11 the West has begun to
speak plainly, even under threat of a fatwah,
about what they perceive to be the absurdities of the Muslim view of paradise. After
9/11 every American whose brain was not
wrapped in duct tape soon learned that the
non-Iraqi Muslim fundamentalist murderers
who piloted the planes were anticipating sex
with seventy-two dark-eyed virgins in paradise. (Nowhere does the Qur'an mention
the number of virgins, but then how many
Christians can recite the gospel truth about
their heaven?)

On June 9, 2006 *The New York Post*
ran a picture, on the front page, of the dead
head of Al Zarqawi, the murderous Al Qaeda

headhunter, with a cartoon bubble coming out of his *rigor mortis* mouth: "Warm up the virgins." In the West the undercurrent and outpouring of ridicule of Muslim paradise has not stopped, nor will it ever, if Qur'an-thumpers do not stop blowing themselves up in the hope of entering paradise. Of course, we Americans, led by neoconservative imperialists, have been doing some blowing up ourselves. We do not use suicide bombers. We don't need to, because we have cruise missiles, stealth bombers, superhornets, and warthogs. It takes a lot of Muslim martyrs to equal one well-placed cluster bomb. At least when Muslims blow themselves up, their god, Allah—through the angel Gabriel—has promised more than a sketchy nondescript dwelling. Coincidentally, Jesus would know the angel Gabriel because he/she/it is the same angel who told his mother that Jesus had quickened inside of her. (See Da Vinci's painting of *The Annunciation* for an authentic picture of the angel Gabriel.)

According to an American president we are now engaged in the mother of all religious wars against Islamofascists, not to be confused with the Christofascists such as our own Lieutenant General Boykin, Deputy Undersecretary of Defense for Intelligence. He proclaims: "We in the army of God, in the house of God, kingdom of God, have been raised for such a time as this." [19] Joy to the world. This so-called War on Terror, the mother of all misnomers, is "like totally awesome", if you are a Christian televangelist or a Muslim mullah giddily hoping for the big rapture in the sky. But what if you are neither?

Perhaps *New York Post* non-politically-correct ridicule is what we non-thumpers

need to jump-start thumper brains into think-
ing critically about their ancient religious
myths, which are having so much deadly
impact on our twenty-first century lives. Per-
sonally, I would prefer the gospel according
to Monty Python as a means for converting
small Muslim and Christian fundamentalist
minds to reason. But whether it is ultimately
by ridicule, humor, or rational intellectual
discourse (though that is inherently prob-
lematic with people who believe in
unprovable myths) that the absurdities of our
religious beliefs are challenged, I agree with
Harris that it must begin immediately. Why?
Because Christian fundamentalists, Muslim
fundamentalists and Jewish fundamentalists[20] are ready, willing, and now more than
ever in the history of mankind quite able
to blow us all up, because their messianic
beliefs and desire for apocalypse now.

In recent history no two men have had more impact on the course of world events than George W. Bush and Osama bin Laden. Other than the fact that one has a beard and one does not; one is extremely clever and one is not, they really do have a number of personal things in common. Both were born into very wealthy families. Both have had strained relationships with their powerful fathers. Both claim to be believers in apocalyptic religions.[21] Both rely heavily on believers in apocalyptic religions for their political power.[22] Both believe in an afterlife. Both claim to talk to God—and don't forget Tony "that fine Christian" Blair, too. (Two Aussies who don't watch *Fox News* told me about him.) Both have cast their respective wars in religious terms. Muslims have Qur'an quoting "rag heads" —as our Christian enlisted men often refer to them—

lined up to die for Allah. Americans have onward Christian soldiers lined up to die for Jesus. As Lieutenant General William Boykin "gave witness" when discussing a Muslim warlord in Somalia, "I knew that my God was bigger than his. I knew that my God was a real God and his was an idol." [23] (What does it mean Dr. Freud—this dream that my God's gun is bigger than their god's gun?)[24]

After 9/11 Billy Graham's son, Franklin "Cracker" Graham, announced on *CNN* that we should "nuke 'em"—the Muslims that is. ("Blessed are the peacemakers for they shall be called the sons of God," Matthew 5:9. Graham's a selective reader of the Bible just like Grandpa.) One of the loving legacies that Jerry Falwell left behind is "Liberty", the Christian university he founded. There, according to *Newsweek*, his followers are training Christian debaters, who can perform "assault ministry." [25] (To assault whom? Me, Muslims, or both?) After Israel invaded southern Lebanon in the summer of 2006, Christian fundamentalists declared support for the killing. (Once again ignoring Jesus' beatitude about that whole peacemaker thing, apparently believing that none of the children killed were "unborn.") The Right-Reverend John Hagee of Texas called the Israeli invasion "a battle between good and evil" and said support for Israel was "God's foreign policy." [26] What Christian fundamentalists like Hagee soft peddle is their belief that when their god flies down from the clouds in the Second Coming, even Israeli-Jews, who collaborated with the Christians, will be thrust into a fiery hell as non-believing sinners.

Yet another political operative cloaked

as clergy, D. James Kennedy of the Coral Ridge Ministries, sets out the evangelicals' theo-fascist agenda: "Our job is to reclaim America for Christ, whatever the cost. We are to exercise godly dominion and influence over our neighborhoods, our schools, our government, our literature and arts, our sports arenas, our entertainment media, our news media, our scientific endeavors—in short over every aspect and institution of human society." [27]

In the final analysis those fine Christian Americans, who applaud a preemptive war foreign policy and an every-sperm-is-sacred domestic policy, do so based upon their zealous belief in a Christian afterlife. While articulating his judicial philosophy at the University of Chicago Divinity School, U.S. Supreme Court Justice Antonin "Opus Dei" Scalia made this revealing point: "For the

believing Christian, death is no big deal." [28]
His revelation not only explains why Scalia
was not afraid to go duck hunting with Mr.
Cheney before he ruled on Dick's "energy
task force" case before him in the Supreme
Court, it also speaks legions why, after a few
crocodile tears, American-flag-draped cof-
fins and pictures of maimed Muslim children
are no big deal for those Christian zealots,
who diverted us from the evil delivered by
bin Laden and led us into the temptation of a
war in Iraq.

    As an agnostic for most of my adult life
I was content to quietly, hopefully peace-
fully, live my life and teach my children
based on what Esther and Hillel had distilled
from all the biblical commentary. However,
Christians—like their Muslim cousins—
are increasingly becoming a threat to life,
liberty, and the pursuit of happiness in this

life. Muslim fundamentalists want a global Muslim theocracy. Christian fundamentalists want a global Christian theocracy.[29] That is bad enough, but they are all prepared to take the rest of us to an early grave to get their mission accomplished. To borrow from the self-righteous Supreme Court justice, who has more influence on our lives than any non-lawyer would be expected to know: "For believing Muslims and Christians death is no big deal, because they know where they are going." [30]

Well I for one do not know where I am going, or if I am going. In any event I would prefer not to go to the desolate heaven Jesus described. If I were forced to make a choice between the Christian heaven Jesus described in the Gospels and the Muslim heaven relayed by Gabriel in the Qur'an, I'd opt to go with the Muslims. A Moroccan friend in Denver raves about the wine he expects to drink in his paradise. From Allah to the archangel Gabriel to the Prophet Muhammad, Muslims can claim a more detailed portrait of heaven which included much more than an austere house.

Comparing heaven according to Jesus with heaven according to Allah is like comparing a Motel 6 with a Ritz or a Four Seasons. For one thing, heavenly bound Muslims are promised eternal lodging, not in an austere house, but in palaces with luscious gardens. "Gardens graced with flowing streams, and palaces too" (sura 25:10). "For those who fear [the time when they will] stand before their Lord there are two gardens (sura 55:46). "With shading branches" (sura 55:48). "There are two other gardens, below these two." (sura 55:62); "Both of deepest green" (sura 55:64).

While we lack enough fresh-clean drinking water for almost a third of the world's population, not to worry about water in the next life. In the Qu'ran paradise flows with more pure water than the Great Lakes Basin before the white man came. "Here is a picture of the Garden promised to the pious: rivers of water forever pure" (sura 47:15). "With a pair of gushing springs" (sura 55:66). "God will admit those who believe and do good deeds to Gardens graced with flowing streams (sura 47:12).

The Qu'ran will sooner set a worldly traveler dreaming of a place of luxury. "There they will be comfortably seated on soft chairs" (sura 18:31). "They will sit on couches upholstered with brocade" (sura 55:54). "They will all sit on green cushions and fine carpets" (sura 55:76). Whether "off the rack" or "custom made," fashion

statements can be made in Muslim heaven.
"There they will be adorned with bracelets
of gold. There they will wear green gar-
ments of fine silk and brocade" (sura 18:31).

Unlike Jesus, who did not even promise
eternal matzoh ball soup, Allah told the angel Gabriel, who told Mohammed that Allah
promised that the Muslim heaven has abundant food and elegant table settings. "Dishes
and goblets of gold will be passed around
them with all that their souls desire and their
eyes delight in. There you will remain: this
is the Garden you are given as your own,
because of what you used to do, and there
is abundant fruit in it for you to eat" (sura
43:71-73). "[T]he fruit of both gardens
within easy reach" (sura 55:54). There are
also "rivers of milk and honey" (sura 47:15).
For the departed, who remain health conscious, the Muslim heaven offers antioxidant

pomegranates. "With fruits—date palms and pomegranate trees" (sura 55:68). And, like the chocolate in Willy Wonka's Chocolate Factory, the wine "runs in rivers" (sura 47:15).

Finally, of course, there is that whole "hey you get off of my cloud" sex thing. There is nothing that makes Christians with their celibate heaven more apoplectic or more disparaging of Islam than the promise that Muslim's are rewarded with sex in heaven. Muslim men, like Mormon men before they gained statehood for Utah, can bring as many wives as possible to heaven. "Enter Paradise, you and your spouses: you will be filled with joy" (sura 43:70). "There will be maidens restraining their glances" (sura 55:56). "There are good-natured beautiful maidens...Dark-eyed, sheltered in pavilions...Untouched beforehand by man

or jinn" (sura 55:70, 72, 74). A wife here.
A bodacious virgin there. What is a fellow
to do for eternity? For that matter what is a
Muslim woman suppose to do for eternity?
Those perplexing questions aside; the need
for multiple gardens should be patently
obvious.

In stark contrast to the sexual oppor-
tunities awaiting in Muslim paradise, Jesus
talked only about the physical transfigura-
tion of wives and husbands at the time of the
resurrection. Again, whether that resurrection occurs immediately after Christians
die or only after Jesus returns in the Second
Coming, remains unsettled by the Gospels.
What is certain is that the afterlife described
by Jesus is celibate as hell. Reciting the law
of Moses, the skeptical Sadducees asked
Jesus, "who lives with whom" after the resurrection that he so heralded:

Now there were seven brothers among
us; the first married, and died childless,
leaving the widow to his brother. The
second did the same, so also the third
down to the seventh. Last of all, the
woman herself died. In the resurrection,
then, whose wife of the seven will she be?
For all of them had married her
(Matthew 22:25-28).

In the Broadway musical "Jesus Christ Su-
perstar" a smitten Mary Magdalene singing
the Andrew Lloyd Webber and Tim Rice
show stopping tune "I Don't Know How to
Love Him" hinted that the Jesus character had
a modicum of romantic tingling or inkling.
However, according to the "Off Broadway"
Gospels and not those nasty Gnostic gospels,
the literal Jesus of the New Testament could

never have been cast in such a role. A true
romantic heterosexual would have answered
the Sadducees' question with a question,
as Jesus so often did; perhaps responding:
"Who of the seven loved this woman the
most and who of the seven did this woman
love the most? Such love by a man for a
woman and by a woman for a man shall
endure eternally for all, who believe in me."
Instead the asexual Jesus of the Gospels
eliminated the holy sacrament of marriage
and thereby threw sex out of heaven altogether. "Jesus answered them [the Saddu-
cees], 'You are wrong, because you know
neither the scriptures nor the power of God.
For in the resurrection they neither marry
nor are given in marriage, but are like angels
in heaven'" (Matthew 22:29-30).

      Whether there be an angelic kama
sutra or not; most intellectually honest

humans will concede that what the Muslim
god described as heaven in his "good" book
sounds more inviting than what the Christian
god described as heaven in his "good" book.
The Muslim heaven offers everything that
Jesus offered and more. In Muslim heaven
you still get the bonus package of Abraham,
Isaac, and Jacob (sura 38:45), and Jesus will
be there, too (sura 4:163)! For an insular
people—post–great Moorish culture—with
bleak educational and economic opportuni-
ties in Muslim dominated countries, the
Muslim afterlife represents a surreal entice-
ment for martyrdom. At least, it sure beats
hanging around for eternity in the Christian
heaven with some cherubs and three old
patriarchs,[31] staring at seventy names with
a parched mouth, not knowing whether you
would ever get something to eat or drink and
not one woman, virgin or otherwise, in sight.

But, I do not want to go to the Muslim heaven either. The whole virgin thing is way over-rated. Having been a virgin once myself, I would find it all too awkward. Also, having that Lexington & Concord freedom thing somehow embedded in my DNA simply does not fit with having some black-robed Qu'ran-chanting ayatollah telling me what to think, what to read, or how to live. Admittedly in recent history the United States has experienced an alarmingly virulent metastasis of judges in both federal and state courts, like Scalia and Clarence "Cruel & Unusual" Thomas, who vote to execute the mentally retarded, eliminate the right to habeas corpus and voice a high pitched political preference for us all to pray to their god Jesus. However, even such black robed Christian fundamentalist judges can not yet shred Americans under The

Bill of Rights quite as fast as black robed
Muslim mullahs can shred anybody under
Sharia–Muslim religious law–for naming
Teddy Bears "Mohammed." And the Muslim
idea of respect for women would not work
well in my family. As my daughter quips in
response to a certain genre of sexist jokes,
"At least blondes don't wear burquas."

The Truth

The god awful truth is that when two thousand years of commentary are washed away, Jesus' description of heaven is so pathetically meager as to leave only three choices:

A. The Christian heaven is a sterile place devoid of color, texture and anything fun to do for eternity;

B. Jesus was a carpenter not a visionary designer and did a hell of a lousy job describing the Christian heaven;

C. Jesus had never been to any Christian heaven, which means he is not the man-god Constantine claimed.

The truth is "C." If our magnificent, but fragile Earth was created by a god, an all knowing and all powerful god, he/she/it would never have designed the drab and desolate afterlife Jesus described in the Gospels. However, you may draw your own conclusion, while we still have freedom from religion in parts of the world. In the meantime, I have done what Christians have been doing for two thousand years. I have made up my own non-gospel version of heaven.

I want to live forever with my wife and children in a cottage beside a clear lake where no acid rain falls, no jet skis roar, and pregnant women can eat the perch and the lake trout. I want to learn how to play a piano, like Bill Murray in *Groundhog Day*. I want a big library of books and music for Frost-like snowy evenings during winter solstice. I want to have my friends (and yes,

my mother-in-law with that spoiled-brat cat)
stop by from no-time to no-time to watch the
summer sunsets. I want my mom and dad to
meet their two grandchildren. I want all the
dogs I have ever owned to run around like
puppies in Renee's garden of wildflowers,
chasing butterflies. And every day I want
all the children I have ever represented with
cerebral palsy to ride by on their very own
bicycles, laughing, waving, and throwing
maize and blue water balloons at my old
rusty mailbox. And don't forget the wine.

Appendix
Letter to Churches

September 11, 2006

Dear Reverend,

I am doing research for a book on Christian theology, specifically the description of Heaven in the words of Jesus Christ. The focus of my writing is not about how one gets to Heaven (ie. Truly, I tell you, whoever does not receive the kingdom of God as a little child will never enter it. Luke 18:17). My current area of interest is not about the obstacles to entering Heaven (ie. Truly I tell you, it will be hard for a rich person to enter the kingdom of heaven. Matthew 19:23). Nor is my work focusing upon any Books of the Old Testament, the disciples or St. Paul; nor any of the great Christian theological writers, Origen, Augustine, Aquinas, whoever your preference may be.

My area of interest is not on what anyone
but Jesus said to describe Heaven. Simply
put: what is Jesus' description of Heaven?

I am using the word "description" as
one of my Webster's defines it: "discourse
intended to give a mental image of something experienced (as a scene, person or sen-
sation)." So as not to skew your response
I will not suggest any of the passages from
the Gospels (or anywhere else) where Jesus
describes Heaven, but point out solely for
purpose of example that the Qur'an gives as
one of its descriptions of Heaven/Paradise—
"they will have Gardens of lasting bliss
graced with flowing streams."

If in answering my question you rely
upon any of the parables of Jesus, please
note and comment which of the Parables
of Jesus you believe offer descriptions of
the Kingdom of Heaven as distinguished

from the Kingdom of God or what Joachim
Jeremias, the former Emeritus Professor of
New Testament in the University of Gottin-
gen, called the Parousia parables or parables
of the Second Coming. For purpose of my
research I am primarily using the Revised
Standard Version and the NRSV. If you rely
on any Gospels other than those recognized
in the RSV or NRSV please so indicate.

    I have some appreciation for how busy
your ministry probably is. If time does not
permit you to answer this inquiry, would you
please consider designating a representa-
tive, who would fairly represent the views of
your church or parish in responding to my
question. Any response that I receive will
constitute permission to use that response
and all of its contents, including but not
limited to the name of your church and name
of the person responding, in my book and

any other ancillary productions or media,
which may result therefrom. Any response
that I receive will also constitute a waiver by
you/the responder to any royalties or other
compensation that may possibly result from
the publication of my work and your re-
sponses. (I apologize for these legalisms, but
you know what Jesus said about lawyers.)

Thank you for your anticipated cooperation.

Sincerely,
Jack Beam

The Notes

1.   In *Hein v. Freedom From Religion
Foundation, Inc.*, 2007 U.S. LEXIS 8512,
June 25, 2007 the U. S. Supreme Court dese-
crated our Constitutional prohibition against
Establishment of Religion: "Congress shall
make no law respecting an establishment of
religion." Promoting the Republican political agenda to eliminate the separation of
church and state, President Bush authorized
"faith-based" groups to receive federal tax
dollars. In a 5-4 decision the Republican
controlled high court held that American
taxpayers have no standing/no right to
challenge Mr. Bush's use of our tax dollars
for religious purposes. So much for James
Madison's declaration that "the government
in a free society may not force a citizen to
contribute three pence" for the support of
any religion. How wonderful is it to have
a Muslim cleric in Dearborn, Michigan or

Newark, New Jersey receive tax dollars for his local mosque to promote jihad against Christians? Or do our Christian "strict constructionist" Supreme Court Justices assume that our tax dollars are flowing solely to Christian denominations to promote jihad against Muslims?

2.   "Hello Muddah, Hello Faddah," Allan Sherman & Louis F. Bush, Burning Bush Music, W.B. Music.

3.   Paul Johnson, *A History of the Jews* (Harper Perennial, 1987), 127.

4.   Alan F. Segal, *Life After Death* (Doubleday, 1989), 12.

5.   Op-Ed, *Michigan Daily*, March 29, 2007 as quoting *New York Post*, March 26, 2007.

6.   "Rock 'n' Roll Heaven," Alan O'Day
& John Stevenson, Famous Music LLC;
Sashay Music; W. B. Music, as recorded by
the Righteous Brothers.

7.   Bart D. Ehrman, *Misquoting Jesus*, *The Story Behind Who Changed the Bible and Why* (Harper San Francisco, 2005).

8.   Joachim Jeremias, *The Parables of Jesus* (SCM-Canterbury Press, Ltd., 1954), 230.

9.   Jeremias, 11.

10. "The New Testament, The Great Courses," Bart D. Ehrman, Professor and Chair of Department of Religious Studies, University of North Carolina at Chapel Hill.

11. Falwell funeral streamed on Christian Broadcast News May 22, 2007: www.cbn.com/cbnnews/162473.aspx.

12. Falwell funeral streamed on Christian Broadcast News May 22, 2007: www.cbn.com/cbnnews/162473.aspx.

13. Bill Condie, "America pays tribute at funeral of Enron fraudster 'Kenny Boy,'" *London Evening Standard*, July 13, 2006, 28.

14. Will Durant, *Caesar and Christ, A History of Roman Civilization and of Christianity from Their Beginnings to A.D. 325* (MJF Books, 1944 & 1971) 663-664.

15. Porky Pig is best known for this signature refrain. However, poetic license has been taken here in deference to Jewish kosher and Muslim halal food law.

16. Bart D. Ehrman, *Misquoting Jesus*.

17. Herbert Krosney, *The Lost Gospel, The Quest for the Gospel of Judas Iscariot* (National Geographic, 2006).

18. Sam Harris, *The End of Faith* (W.W. Norton & Co., 2005), 48.

19. Richard T. Cooper, "General Casts War in Religious Terms: The top soldier assigned to track down Bin Laden and Hussein is an evangelical Christian who speaks publicly of 'the Army of God,'" *Los Angeles Times*, October 16, 2003.

20. It was not a Palestinian, who assas-
sinated the last great Israeli Prime Minister
for supporting the Oslo Peace Accords and a
Palestinian State. It was a messianic Israeli
Jew, who murdered Yitzhak Rabin, "the soldier for peace." Alan Cowell, Assassination
in Israel: The Israeli Right, *New York Times,*
November 7, 1995

21. Segal, "In some ways, Bin Laden's
ideology is not only fundamentalist but
apocalyptic because it seeks to foment a war
of Islam against the West which will end in
the total victory of Islam and the reestab-
lishment of the true Caliphate, as a prelude
eventually for 'the day of judgment' (Yawm
al-Din). This is quite obviously an analogue
to Messianism in Judaism and Christianity." Non-kissing cousins indeed. *Life After
Death*, 689.

22. Johanna Neuman, "Bush's Inaction Over General's Islam Remarks Riles Two Faiths, Muslims call for rebuke of Boykin, but such a move could isolate key Christian supporters." *Los Angeles Times*, November 23, 2003.

23. "General Casts War in Religious Terms."

24. Whether it is Jesus versus Allah, Christian heaven versus Muslim heaven (or Superman versus Spiderman)..."there is something that most Americans share with Osama bin Laden, the nineteen hijackers and much of the Muslim world. We, too, cherish the idea that fantastic propositions can be believed without evidence." Harris 29

25. Susannah Meadows, "Cut, Thrust and Christ," *Newsweek*, February 6, 2006, 56.

26. David D. Kirkpatrick, "For Evangelicals, Supporting Israel Is 'God's Foreign Policy,'" *New York Times*, November 14, 2006, A1 & A6.

27. Abraham H. Foxman, "Religion in America's Public Square: Are We Crossing the Line?" Anti-Defamation League, November 3, 2005, Washington, D.C.

28. Sean Wilentz, "From Justice Scalia, a Chilling Vision of Religion's Authority in America," *New York Times*, July 8, 2002.

29. Kevin Phillips, *Theocracy in America* (Penguin Books, 2006).

30. In *Massachusetts v Environmental Protection Agency*, 127 S. Ct. 1438; 167 L. Ed. 2d 248; 2007 U.S. LEXIS 3785, April 2, 2007, the U.S. Supreme Court voted 5-4 in favor of those of us on the planet who want to fight global warming. The majority held that pollutants, such as carbon dioxide, that cause global warming can be regulated by the government under the Clean Air Act. The four dissenters—Scalia, Thomas, Alito, Roberts—are Christian Bible-thumpers, who could give a starving polar bear about global warming, not because they are "strict constructionists" of the Constitution (which is merely an expedient political cover), but because they believe that Jesus will soon fly down from the clouds in the Second Coming.

31. If Jesus was truly the omniscient and almighty god that Christian's claim, in order to make the Christian heaven more competitive with the Muslim heaven, instead of three humourless Jewish patriarchs he would have promised three consummate Jewish comedians, Groucho Marx, George Burns and Jack Benny.

ABOUT THE AUTHOR

Jack Beam is a graduate of the University of Michigan and Northwestern University School of Law. He has served as both a Staff Attorney for the United States Department of Justice and an Assistant United States Attorney. For the past two decades he has been a partner in Beam & Raymond, a national law firm that represents children with cerebral palsy and other traumatic birth injuries. He and his family live in Chicago.

His first novel, *Go Blue*, has been hailed as "part farce, part fable--a rollicking love story about a harebrained gambling scheme to create a pipeline from the Great Lakes to Las Vegas."